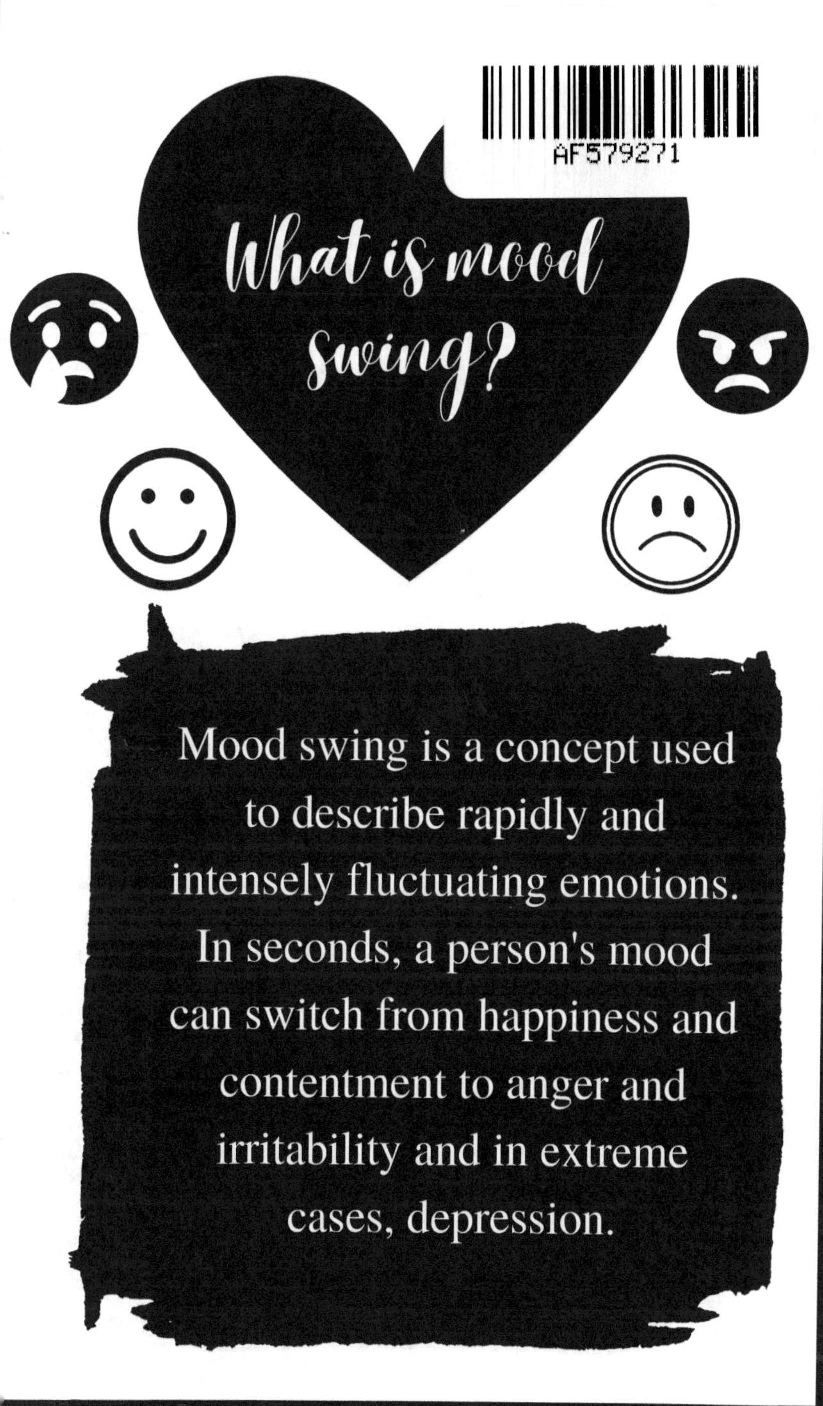
AF579271
What is mood swing?
Mood swing is a concept used to describe rapidly and intensely fluctuating emotions. In seconds, a person's mood can switch from happiness and contentment to anger and irritability and in extreme cases, depression.

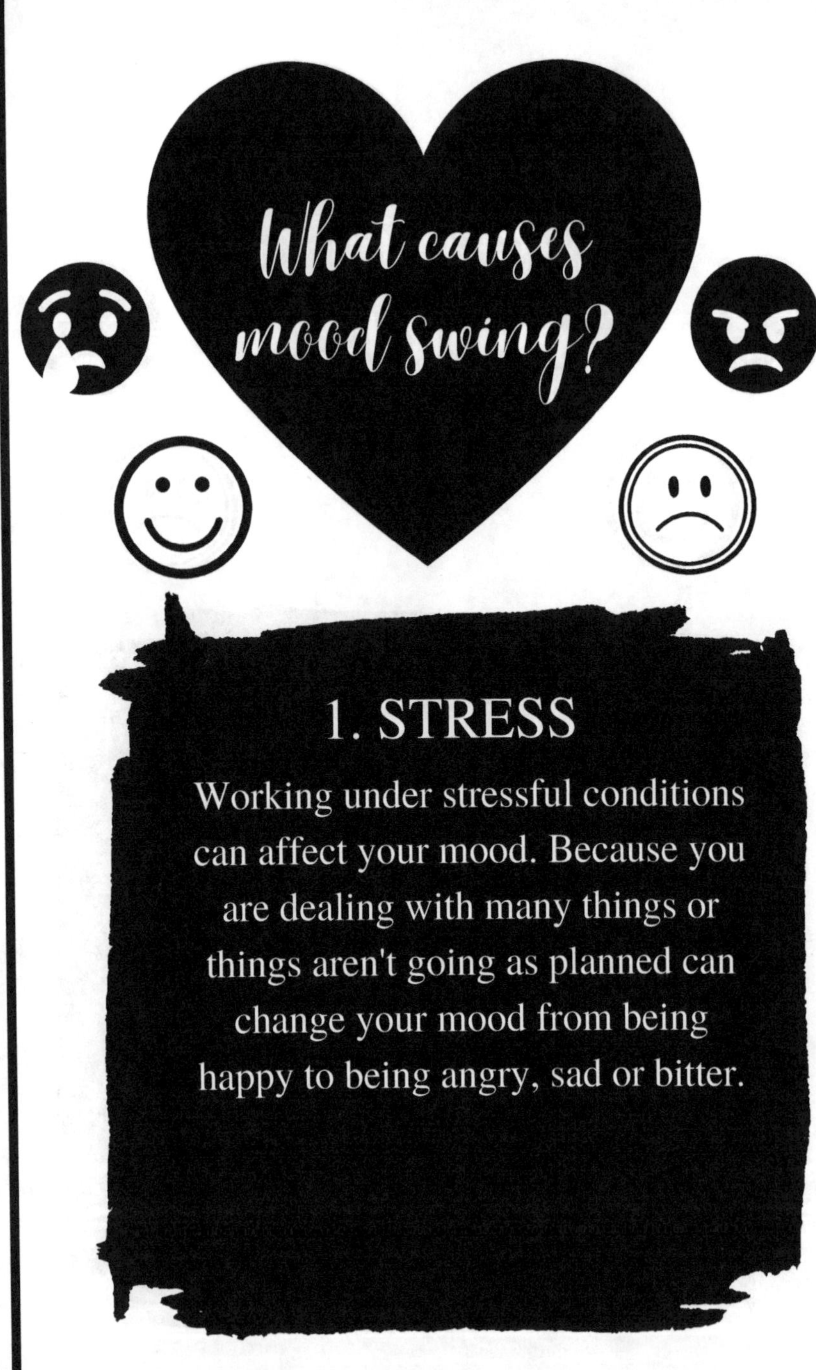

1. STRESS

Working under stressful conditions can affect your mood. Because you are dealing with many things or things aren't going as planned can change your mood from being happy to being angry, sad or bitter.

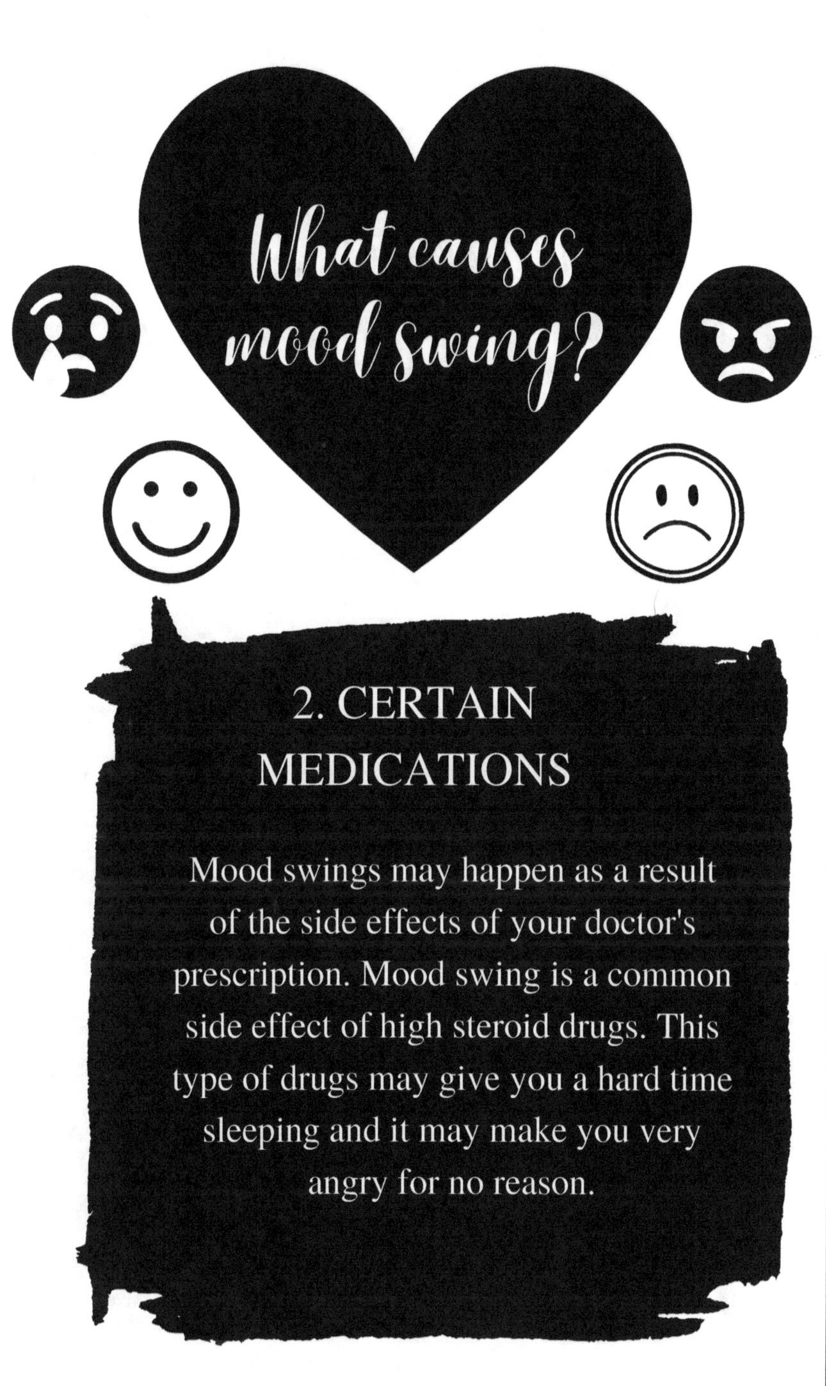
What causes mood swing?
2. CERTAIN MEDICATIONS
Mood swings may happen as a result of the side effects of your doctor's prescription. Mood swing is a common side effect of high steroid drugs. This type of drugs may give you a hard time sleeping and it may make you very angry for no reason.

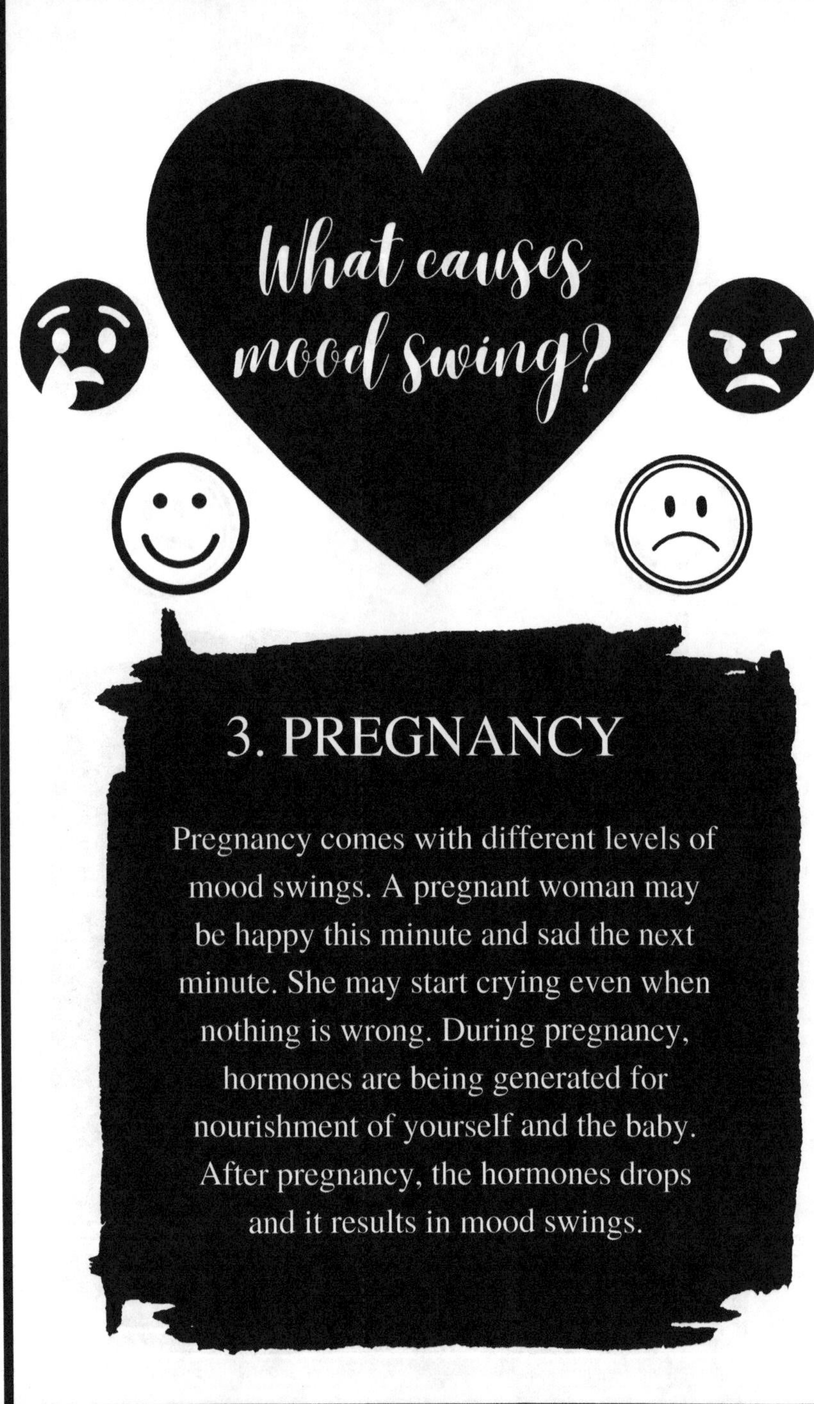
What causes mood swing?
3. PREGNANCY
Pregnancy comes with different levels of mood swings. A pregnant woman may be happy this minute and sad the next minute. She may start crying even when nothing is wrong. During pregnancy, hormones are being generated for nourishment of yourself and the baby. After pregnancy, the hormones drops and it results in mood swings.

What causes mood swing?
4. LACK OF PROPER SLEEP
When you don't sleep fully as you should, your body is not fully refreshed to handle the day's work. In this situation, little things may make you angry or irritate you. This may result in wrong choices which can affect your output and may even lead to depression.

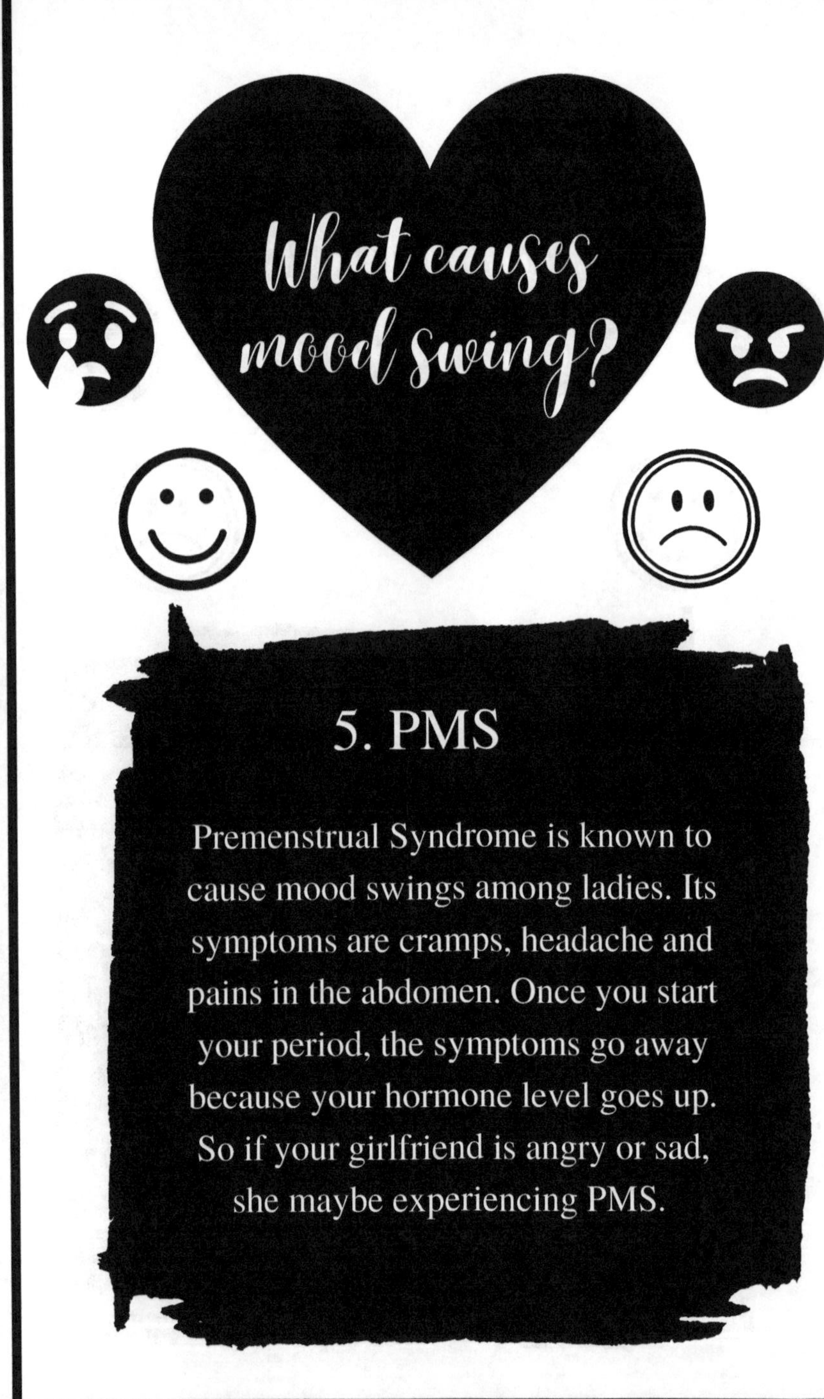

5. PMS

Premenstrual Syndrome is known to cause mood swings among ladies. Its symptoms are cramps, headache and pains in the abdomen. Once you start your period, the symptoms go away because your hormone level goes up. So if your girlfriend is angry or sad, she maybe experiencing PMS.

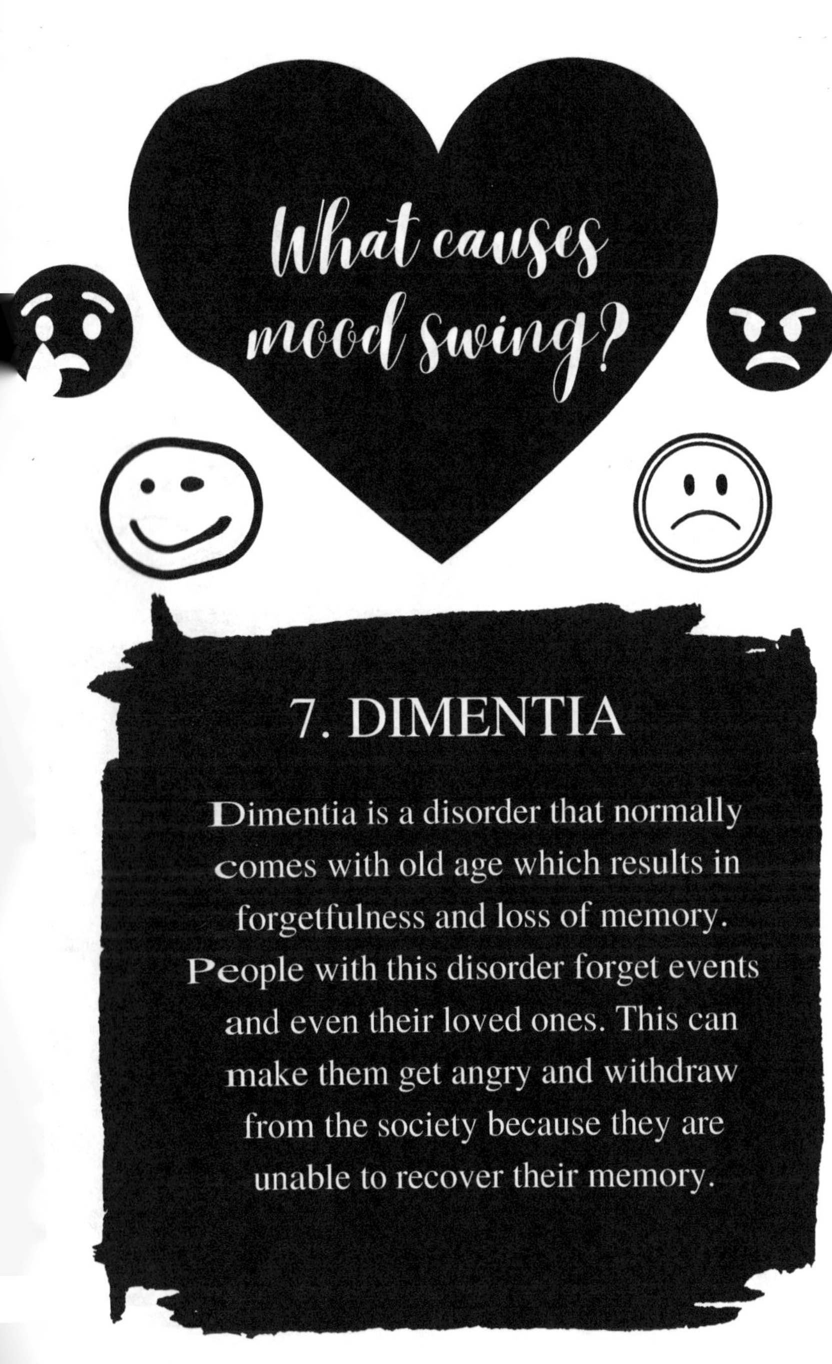

7. DIMENTIA

Dimentia is a disorder that normally comes with old age which results in forgetfulness and loss of memory. People with this disorder forget events and even their loved ones. This can make them get angry and withdraw from the society because they are unable to recover their memory.

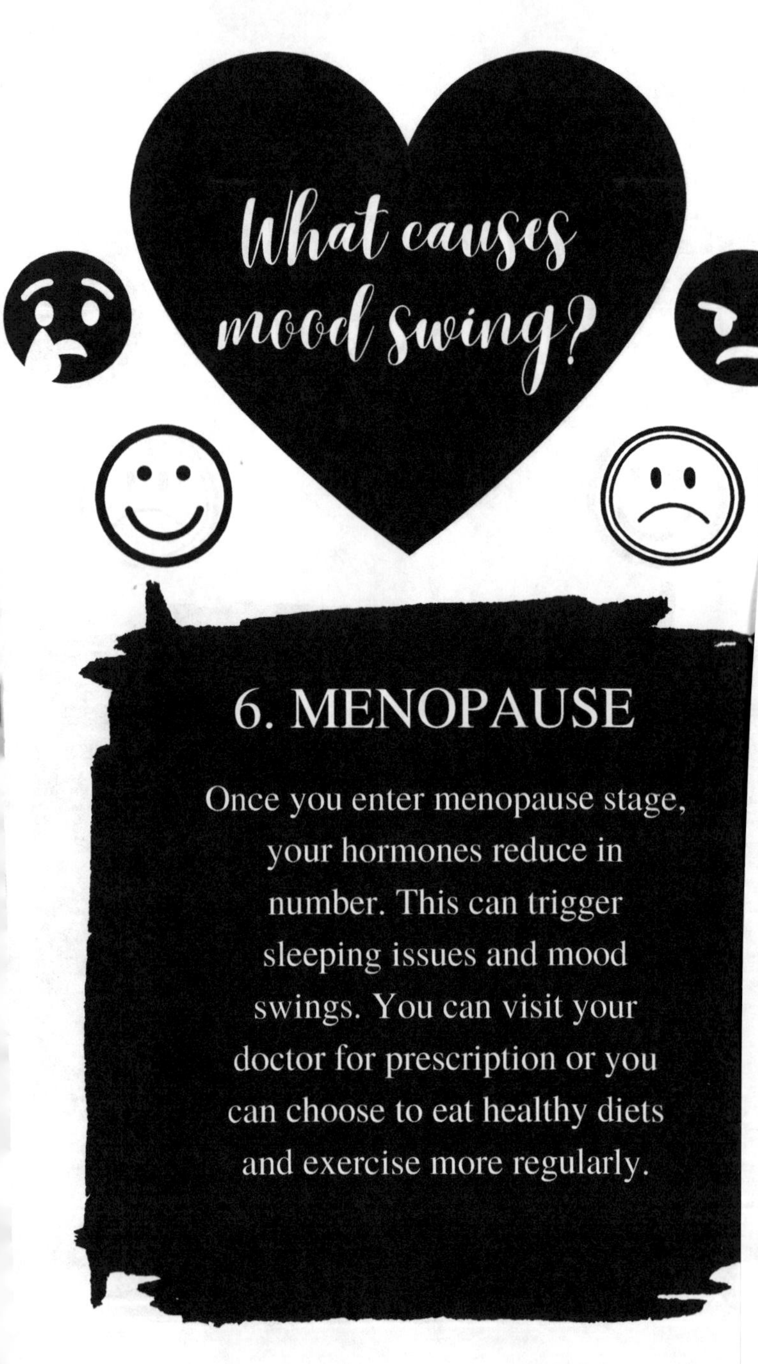

6. MENOPAUSE

Once you enter menopause stage, your hormones reduce in number. This can trigger sleeping issues and mood swings. You can visit your doctor for prescription or you can choose to eat healthy diets and exercise more regularly.

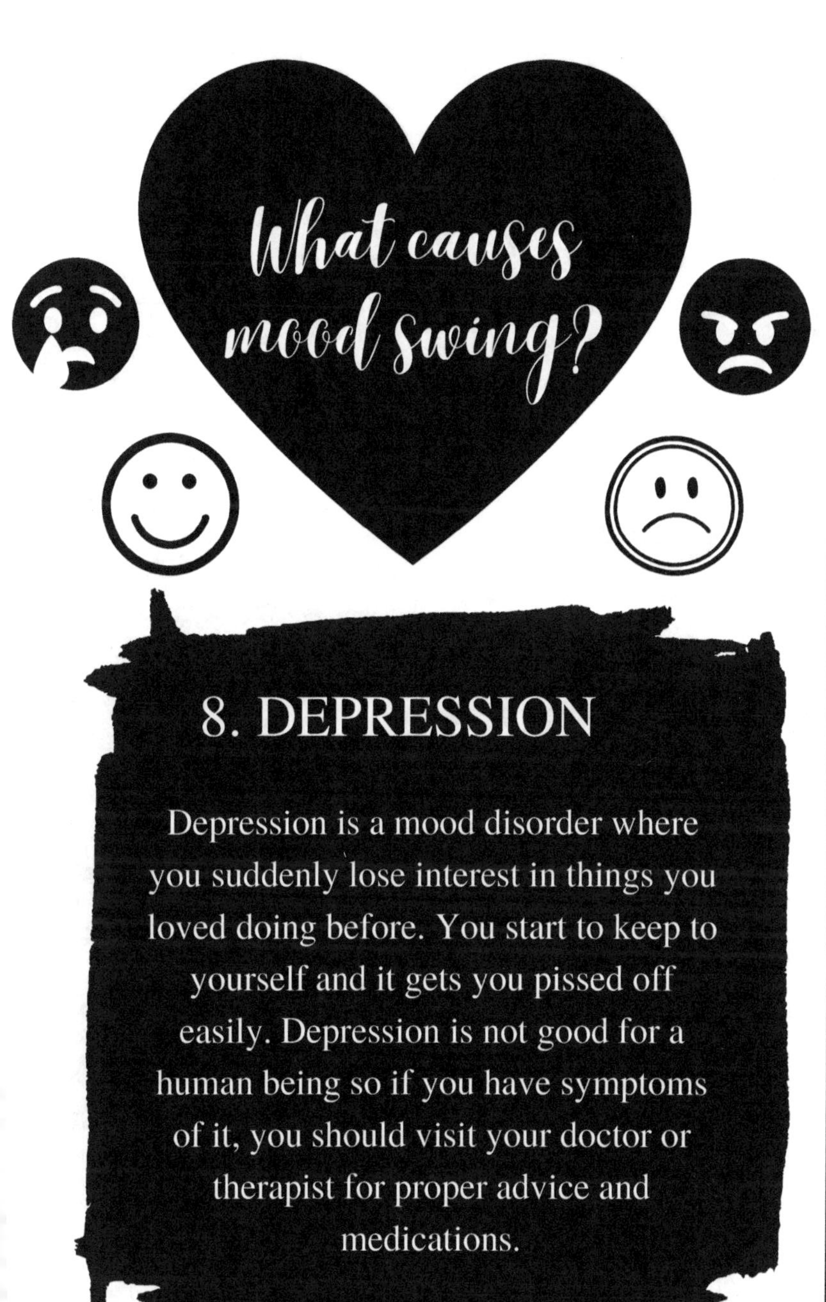

8. DEPRESSION

Depression is a mood disorder where you suddenly lose interest in things you loved doing before. You start to keep to yourself and it gets you pissed off easily. Depression is not good for a human being so if you have symptoms of it, you should visit your doctor or therapist for proper advice and medications.

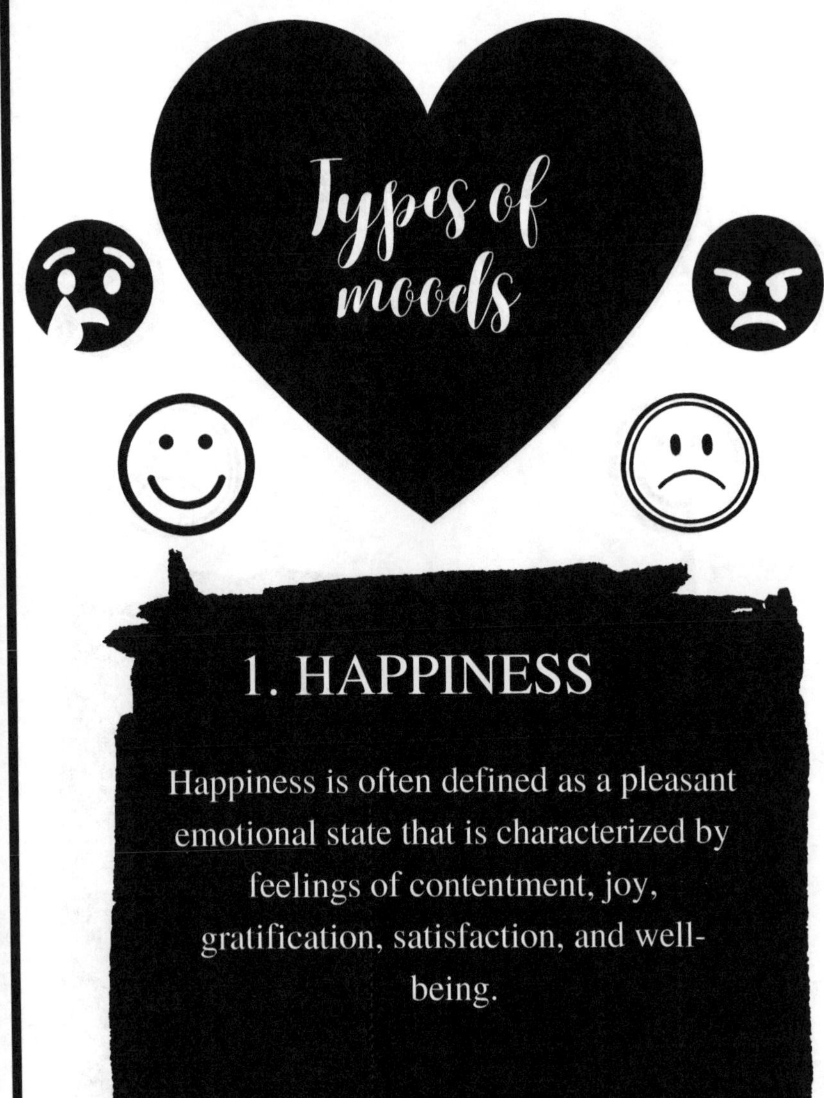

1. HAPPINESS

Happiness is often defined as a pleasant emotional state that is characterized by feelings of contentment, joy, gratification, satisfaction, and well-being.

2. SADNESS

Sadness is another type of emotion often defined as a transient emotional state characterized by feelings of disappointment, grief, hopelessness and disinterest.

3. ANGER

Anger can be a particularly powerful emotion characterized by feelings of hostility, agitation, frustration, and antagonism towards others

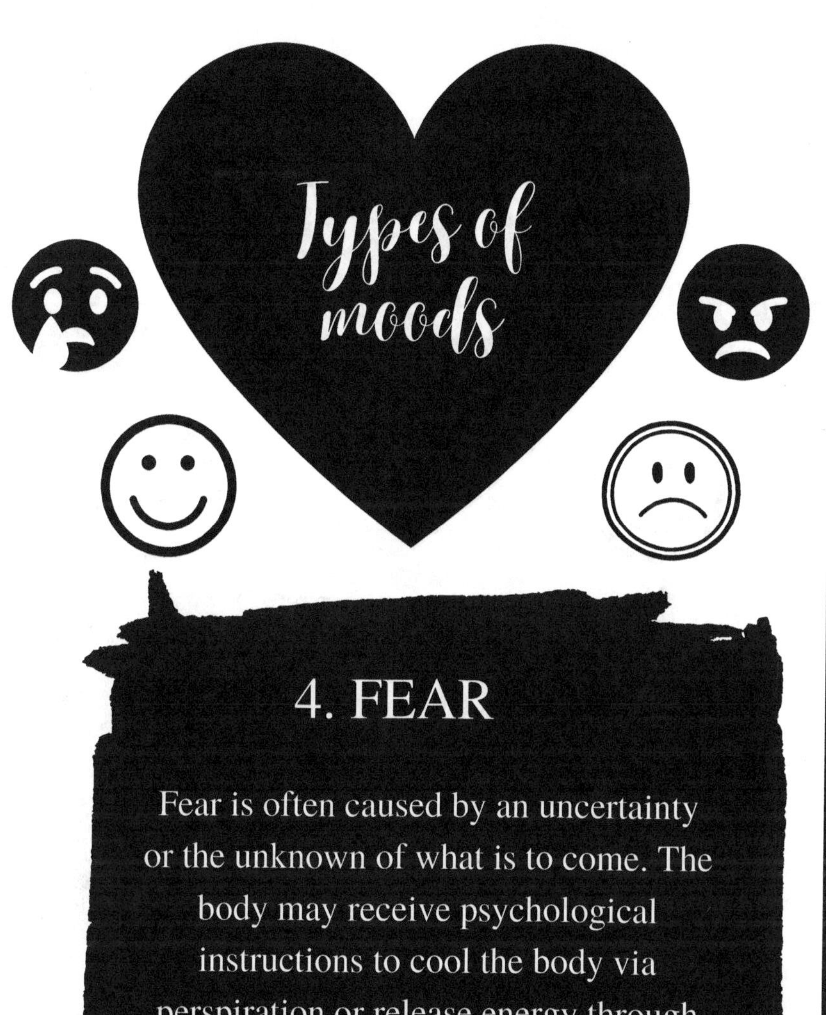

4. FEAR

Fear is often caused by an uncertainty or the unknown of what is to come. The body may receive psychological instructions to cool the body via perspiration or release energy through shaking.

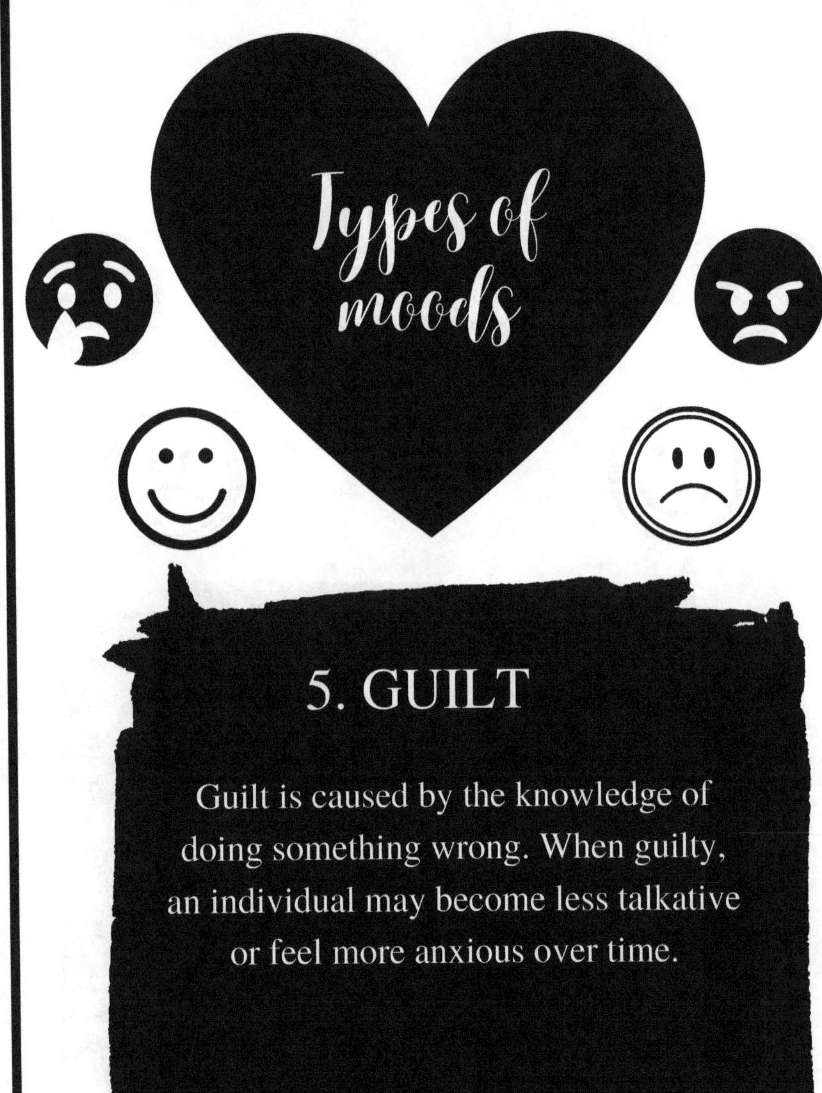

5. GUILT

Guilt is caused by the knowledge of doing something wrong. When guilty, an individual may become less talkative or feel more anxious over time.

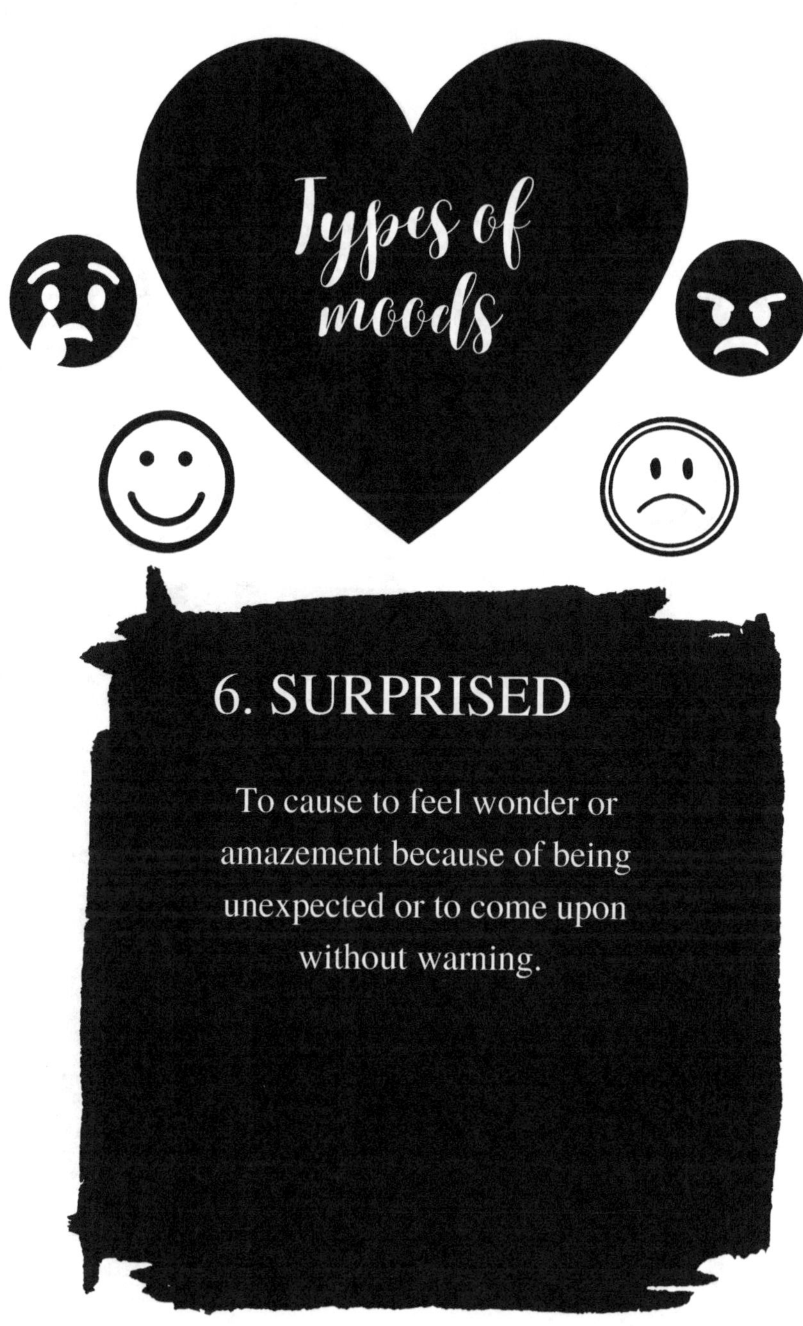
Types of moods
6. SURPRISED
To cause to feel wonder or amazement because of being unexpected or to come upon without warning.

How to deal with mood swing

1. GET SUFFICIENT SLEEP

You need to take your mind of work or school and get a good sleep. Sleep is very important because it nourishes the brain and makes you feel better. Lack of sleep can damage you and change your mood negatively.

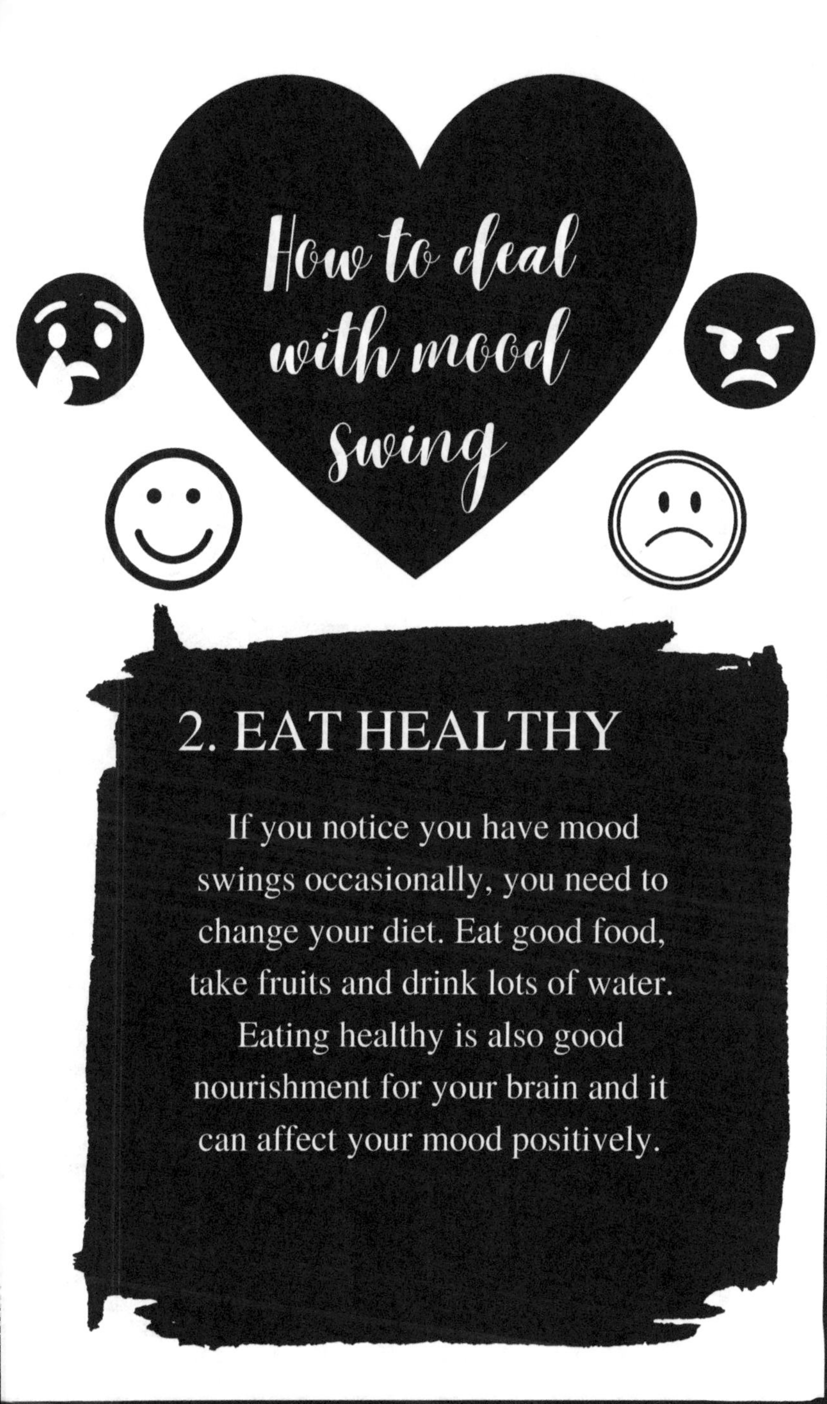
How to deal with mood swing
2. EAT HEALTHY
If you notice you have mood swings occasionally, you need to change your diet. Eat good food, take fruits and drink lots of water. Eating healthy is also good nourishment for your brain and it can affect your mood positively.

How to deal with mood swing
3. AVOID STRESS
Try as much as possible to avoid anything that will stress you. Look for smarter ways to work that will require less work and more output. Even when you are stressed, make sure you take a good shower and sleep very well.

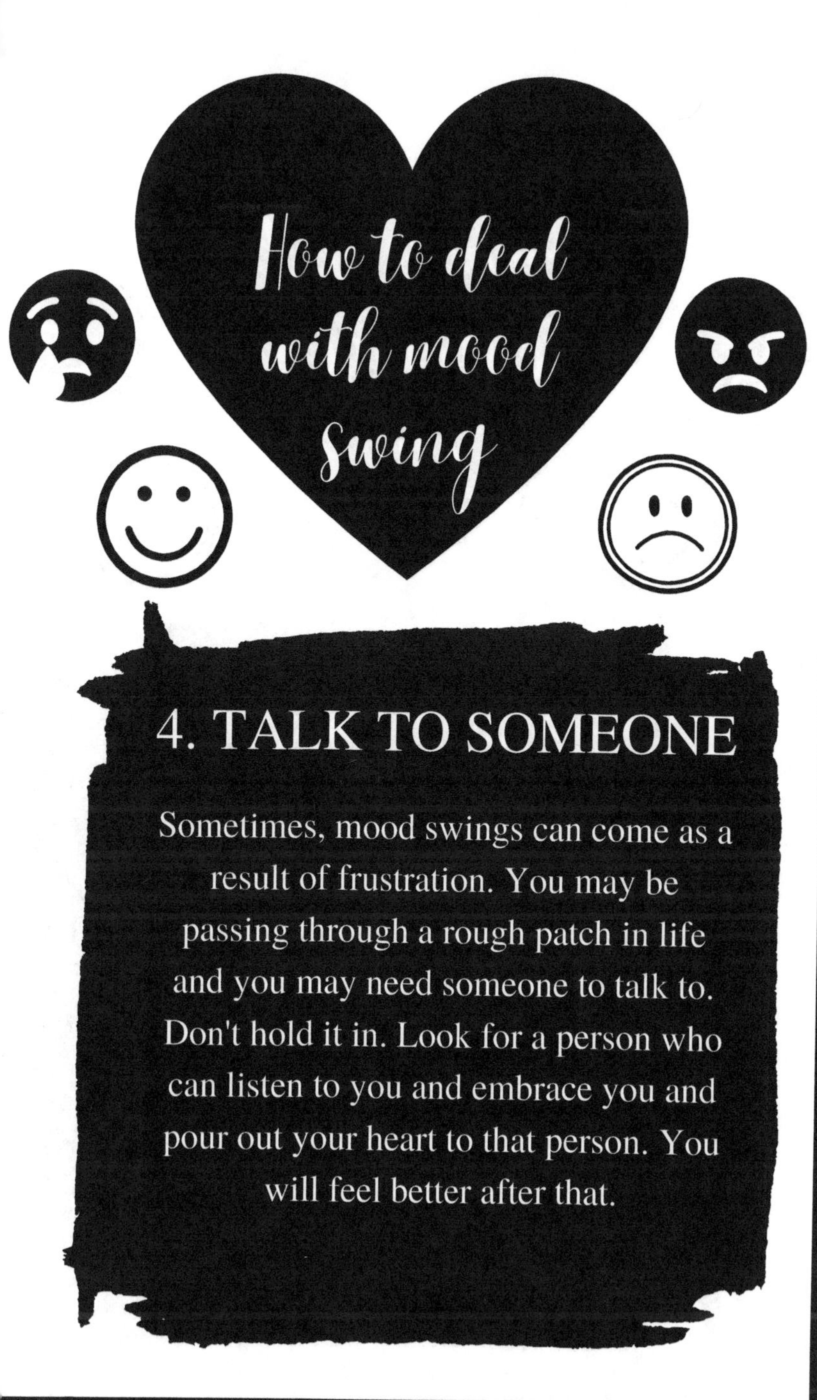

4. TALK TO SOMEONE

Sometimes, mood swings can come as a result of frustration. You may be passing through a rough patch in life and you may need someone to talk to. Don't hold it in. Look for a person who can listen to you and embrace you and pour out your heart to that person. You will feel better after that.

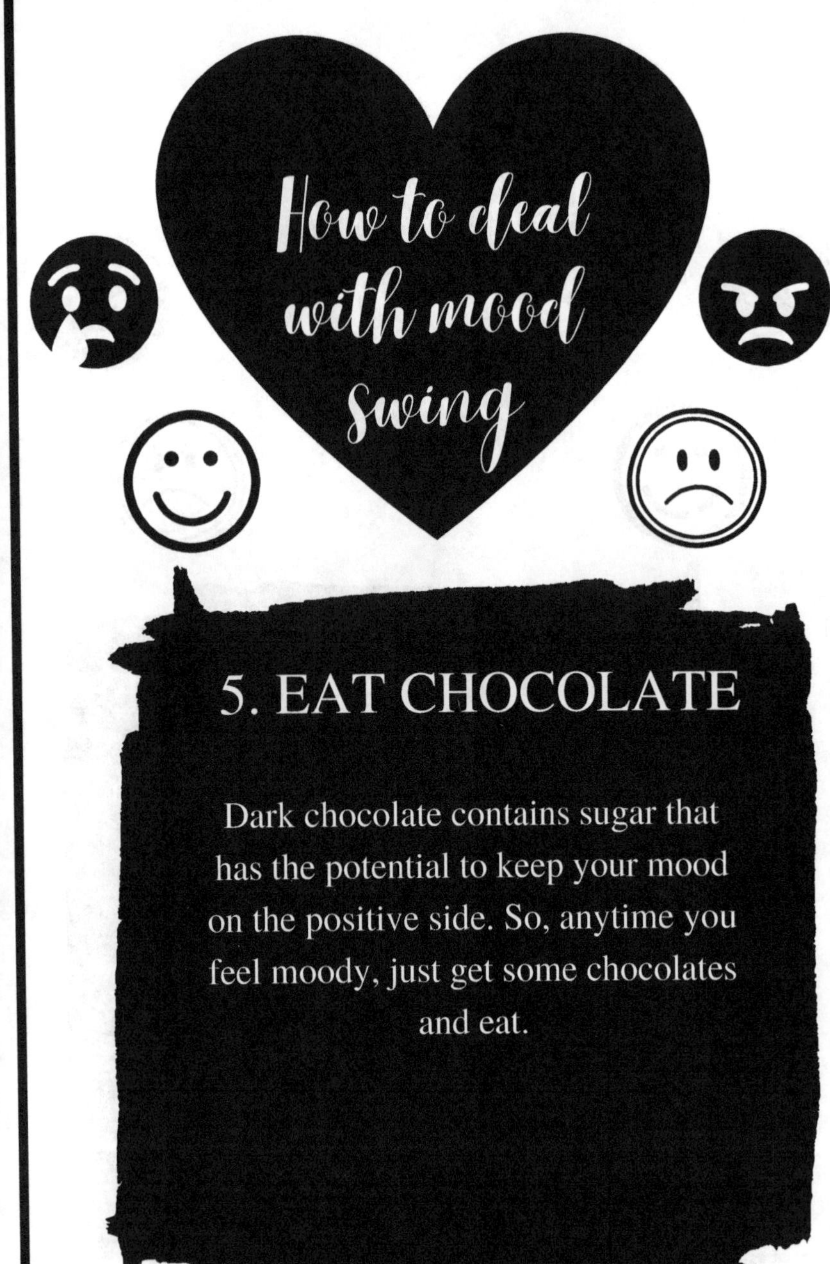

5. EAT CHOCOLATE

Dark chocolate contains sugar that has the potential to keep your mood on the positive side. So, anytime you feel moody, just get some chocolates and eat.

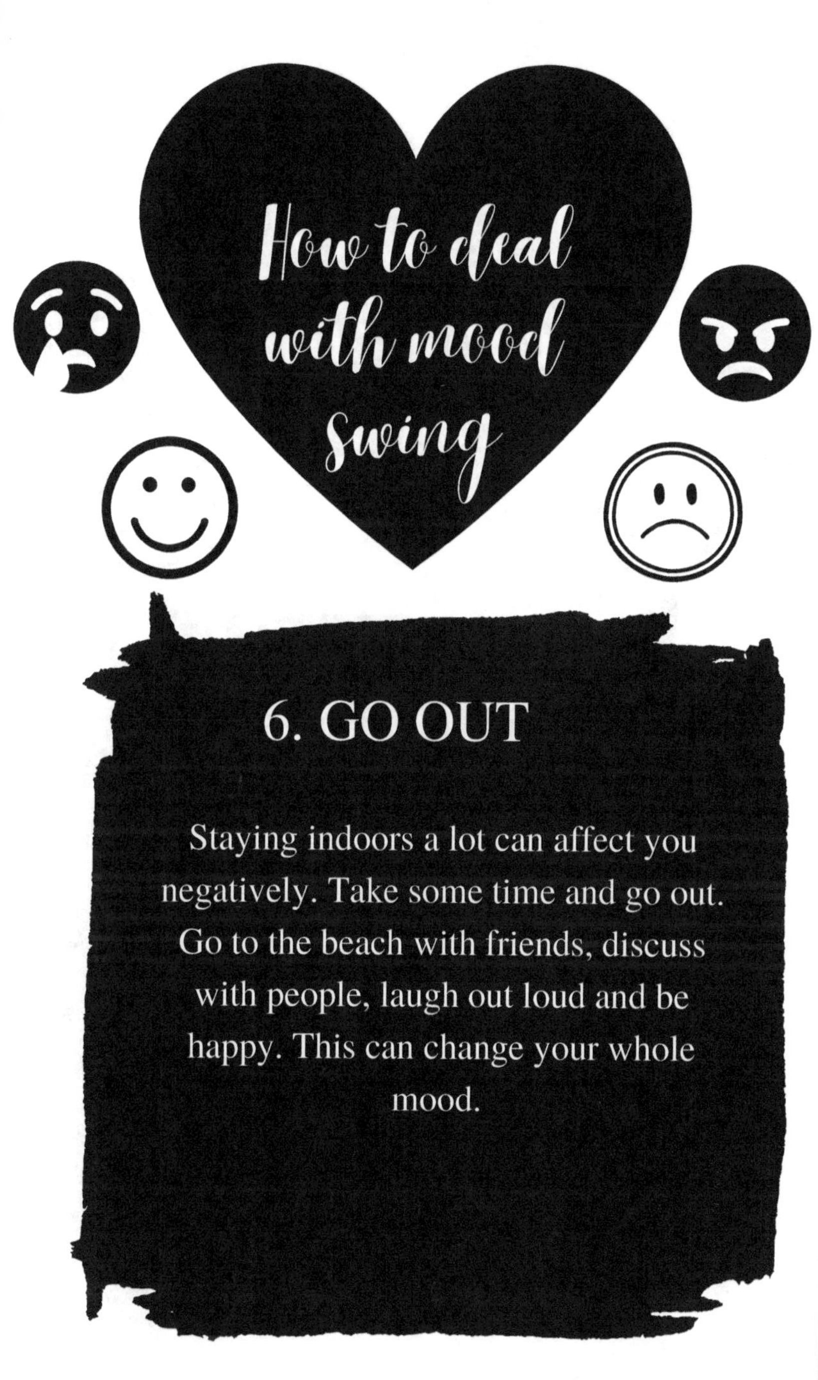

6. GO OUT

Staying indoors a lot can affect you negatively. Take some time and go out. Go to the beach with friends, discuss with people, laugh out loud and be happy. This can change your whole mood.

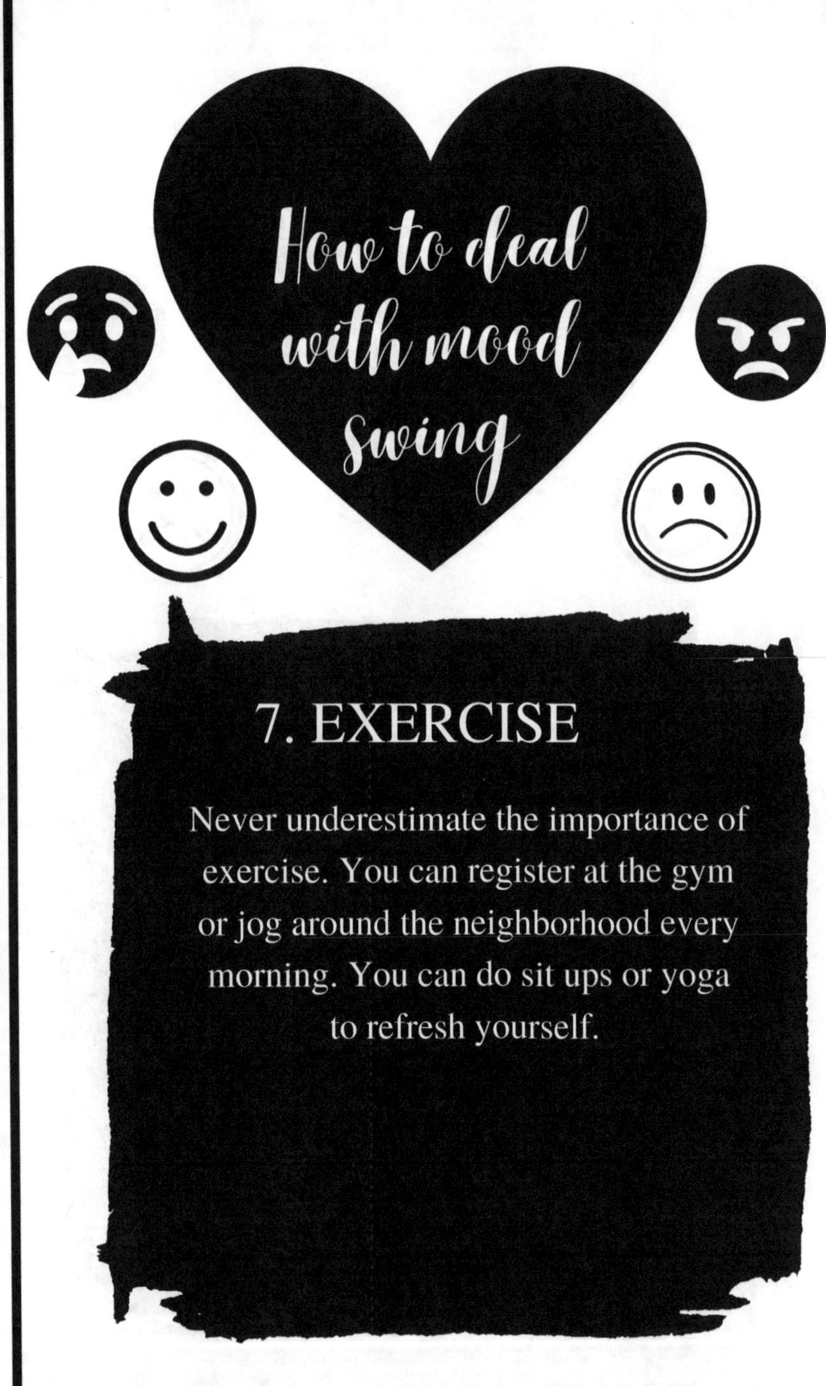

7. EXERCISE

Never underestimate the importance of exercise. You can register at the gym or jog around the neighborhood every morning. You can do sit ups or yoga to refresh yourself.

How to deal with mood swing
8. PLAY WITH FRIENDS OR PETS
You may play fetch with your dog or play with your cat or any of your pets at home. You can also invite your friends for a get-together at your place. Talking to people that you care about can improve your mood swings in unimaginable ways.

Mood swings
Mood swings can happen to anyone, whether young or old, male or female, black or white, tall or short. You just have to learn how to control it when it comes.

www.ingramcontent.com/pod-product-compliance
Lightning Source LLC
LaVergne TN
LVHW010514160826
845677LV00012B/2851

* 9 7 9 8 8 4 4 1 2 5 1 1 9 *